Arrows

Tupelo Press
North Adams, Massachusetts

ARROWS

Poems

Dan Beachy-Quick

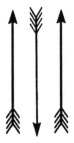

Look at the bow and the lyre.

+

...stepping near...

—Heraclitus, frags. 55 & 122

Table of Contents

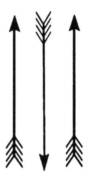

Primer

preface

this book is a learning mist
    in which the hand
        discovers
the thistle it grips—

some texts are forms
    of trespass's
        expectations—
the burr on the cuff

a wandering
    introduction
        to wonder's
barbed dislocations

astronomy

grow shy, grow
    humble, grow
       dense as dying
           star on itself
        collapsing—
    spin darkly to say
I I I your kind
    stutter waits
       for one line
         to break so
       sky tilts, cracks
    and clouds tumble
into the gap

anatomy

an ache   called a school
a palsy   called a pulse
a bone   for curriculum
and for tutor   a ghost

optics

I placed a prism
    in a hole—
this was the day's
    whole lesson—

a rainbow in dirt
    fools convention—
proves the sun not
    wholly a dunce

sitting in the sky's
    far corner—
no idiot split into
    every color's

reflection, but white no-
    thing's complexity
cut open
    for inspection

music

    put down
the crystal
    acorn

    there's
nothing in it
    to see

    there is no
musical, unlovable
    sphere

    clarity
will not ever
    cohere

religion

no outward evidence
    marks the harm within

    but this heat in the hand
inscribed in lines

when prayer denies the heart
    and the mind grows stoic

    a faith-damaged faith
and a faith-damaged damage

ethics

anger, *calm*
    it's only a stone, the mind—
  stone with storm inside—

sorrow, *sing*
    the wren nests in the dead
hollow tree
    and nests in the tedious
heart—

        some pressure pushes
          ore into gem—
        some pressure blows
          open the weed—

love, *press*

prosody

the inner-
      most ex-
cludes
      itself

even it-
      self it
excludes

the eyes
      glance
at a page

all bruised
      the lips
from singing

epistemology

I put my anger in the tree
and smiled at it cunningly
but the wren nested there anyway

I put my sorrow in the hedge
and turned tearful away
but heard the sparrow scratch

in the dirt as the hermit thrush
sang   it sang *worry-no-more*
worry-no-more from the gloom

as it gathered   night fell
from the leaves so calm
I closed in me all my eyes

even memory I closed
and perched myself on this vague
edge called mind

weaving

patience is my lonely prayer
   for both my lovely daughters

practice latching barb to barb
   until the thistle's burrs relent

and as in summer the thrush
   weaves thorns into her nest

let harm work quietly against itself
   until violence is a place for rest

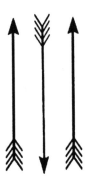

Eidos

I used to eat clouds
When in the motherless air I felt this desire
For thought and the old
Appetites blue underneath their silver
Edge came and the wasp looking for a hole
In the screen made of holes
While rain gains weight at the window
Frame the ever lessening portion
Still mine
            of mind
Called the open sky`

Personae

When I feel sad, I cry.
I put my hands into the holes
Of my eyes and pull out
Reams of blue ribbon
Until my sadness is done.

When I see what I can see
No more, I put my hands
In the holes of my eyes
And unspool the red ribbon
Until blood fills the floor.

The Oracle at—

I dug this hole with my head
Until I forgot I was digging.
I had this idea about myself:
My head a tool for burrowing

Away from myself by digging
Deeper inside. I call the hole
The Library where I study nothing-
ness. Sometimes I have to bury

The system alive to make it die.
Sometimes I have to bury myself
Inside myself to make the facts cry.
Just like infants they do it—

The facts just open their eyes.
Put a coin in the mouth, put
Coins in the eyes. Death
Has a savings account for future

Travel called the mind. Called mind
To mind, but not much was there.
A bush on fire. A chisel. Some stones.
Asterisks where some letters were.

A feeling called a syllable.
Some sense of being alone. Some
Sense of being left alone. No phone,
But buzz of the busy dial tone.

Catullan

Some words some arrows and also wings
Pierce the heart to make it sing
Rug-burns on knees and the back spasm
That crick in the neck from kneeling
To pray with your mouth against the silent
Patch of nerves that delight in possessing
Silence as some form of light so sudden
It blinds the mind that thank you gods
Behind the eyes this light cannot think
I am the flowering weed grazed by every
Passing thing and guess what so are you
That's how the field gets scattered with repair
Longer and longer the shadows grow
Until each one is full grown and has a voice
"Thank you, kid, for all this work,
all this toil, all that plowing, all those songs,
all the root-work that keeps birds in the air
where they belong." Don't call me kid. I'm no kid.
You ghosts in the undergloom always get it wrong.

Theseus's Ship

The wind blows many things off course.
A strong gust tears the winnowed husk in two
Carries the chaff in different directions
One inland and one out to sea.
But different versions mostly end the same.
This story is about a man and a ship.
In Delos he danced a dance the youth still dance.
An imitation of the labyrinth.
The youth still call the dance The Crane.
To dance this dance yourself
Cut from the left side of the head some horns.
Build an altar. It's called the Keraton.
Kerata means "horns." Find a rhythm.
Convolute it. Involute it. Now the dance is done
But the altar remains.
Even when the ship leaves the altar remains.
Sometimes the dance. Often the wind.

*

The thirty-oared galley in which he sailed
Youth to safety they preserved through time.
They took away a timber from time to
Time put it in a pile
They replaced it with a new plank.
Centuries passed and the boat grew younger.
In a thousand years it became new.
Clever or bored some youth looked at the pile
Of old timber and fitting board to board
Built the ship again. They stand side by side

On the long grass the wind blows like waves
When it blows it blows like waves the grass.
Poets and philosophers like to argue
About which ship is Theseus's ship
And which ship is the image or impostor
While the grass rises in swells about their ankles.

*

The thirty-oared galley in which he sailed
Youth to safety they preserved through time.
They took away a timber from time to
Time put it in a pile
They replaced it with a new plank.
Centuries passed and the boat grew younger.
In a thousand years it became new.

Clever or bored some youth looked at the pile
Of old timber and fitting board to board
Built the ship again. They stand side by side
On the long grass the wind blows like waves
When it blows it blows like waves the grass.
Poets and philosophers like to argue
About which ship is Theseus's ship
And which ship is the image or impostor
While the grass rises in swells about their ankles.

*

Kerata

This version blows the labyrinth out to sea.
A strong wind carries the crane off course.
Sometimes one finds the dance winnows the chaff

But mostly yourself remains. A different imitation
Means a different dance, but the rhythm in the head
Calls in the same directions: convolute, involute,
Dance. The youth build the altar. The gust leaves the husk.
And the dance still remains an altar to the tears
A man cut from his side. The youth called the horns "horns."
Many danced this dance when the wind left. Still it is
The story of one ship and some altar: Delos, the Keraton.
Of dance? Often it is about an end. Even now it's done.

The Made Thing Considers Itself

Made the night, made the day, made deep
the waters, made the waters go away,
made the crow and the threshing sound,
made the earth and the shovel, made the dove
and the olive sprig, made holes in the ground
fill up with time, made peace a spring of trouble.
Made the rock, the bone, the mud, the cloud,
the bee-loud glade, made the prayer sound
of water wearing rock away, made the spark,
made the flint, made the dry grass brittle,
made the crystal, made the plug, made memory
on the touch screen glow, made aleph silent,
made fear live at home, made the crosswinds
carry smoke from open window out open door,
made the circuit, made the fire a button turns on,
made the flood, made the drawer, made the deer
on plastic legs in the overgrown lawn,
made paradise, made tears, made the child yawn,

o you, o none, o no one, o you,
o fault, o vault, o stars,
o zero, o rift, o bright sea, o cliff

there is a height, there is a depth, there is
the level ground, there is silence there
where some hear only sound, there is ash
and hair and ashen hair, there is an alphabet
whose last letter wanders in the dust
seeking some thing that can't be found,
there is wisdom and hunger and days,
blank pages in books, music, and strange

animals asleep in beds of their own making
all night these animals dream of themselves
in this world of no proof only evidence.

Some Consequences of the Made Thing

The End. Above these words the sky closes.
It closes by turning white. Not
The white of all clouds or being within a cloud.
White of worldless light. *The End.*
Feel a silence there that reminds you of a scent.
Crushed grass the hooves galloped through
Or is it the binder's glue?
Some silence never not real finally can be
Heard. Silence before the first words.
Precedent chaos. Or marrow work.
Or just the sound of the throat opening to speak.
Like those scholars of pure water
Who rode through mountains and meadows
To drink from each fresh spring a glass
And then with brush and ink wrote poems
On the differences of sameness,
You too feel yourself taste the silent page
Of the end and the silent page of beginning.
They taste so much of whiteness never more
White than white that's been lost.
You have some sense of the book
Altering, page sewn secretly next to page,
Last page stitched to first. O, earth—
It rolls around the solar scroll
Turning nothing into years and years into
Nothing. At *The End* you're a witness to this work
That wears the witness away. And who are you
Anyway. Pronoun of the 2nd person. Lover,
Stranger, God. Student, Child, Shade.
Something similar gathers in you.

Another way of saying I in a poem—
Of saying I in a poem that realizes at the end
That I am just a distance from myself.
And so are you. That same distance.

Song of the—

Vague self who looking ahead says more
Time overflows what it fills but nothing fills it
Birds in uproar and the morning rabbit in the yard
Then it goes quiet and empty as in a dream
When fear and hunger give up the long chase
And death is just a chair in the grass not yet
Assembled
           Then the dream of building time
But the tools make you blush they are so naked
And without shame
              The children keep asking
To sit in your lap every day long after they've grown
Larger than you so large they could if they chose
Make their own chairs out of themselves
                      But they don't
They run through the grass before it's mowed
They run their fingers through the grass and whisper
Into the dirt below keep licking the sun
Keep tricking the worm keep bending your head low
And lower until the blade passes by
                Don't cry
Another thought will grow a head around it
Another word a mouth another moth a moon
Another mote a cloud another atom a sun
Once upon a time in the morning dew
A rabbit left her paw-prints a kind of poem
Written for no one but given to you
               Who are you
Child made mostly of air and dust and water
Who became this walking cloud that speaks out

Loud thoughts the wind blows through your face
Moves you to another place mostly the same
As where you were before a minor elsewhere
Called another day another dream another nap
When you sleep standing up contemplating love
That you love that you love
These consequences of the made thing

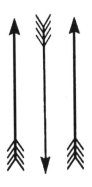

Pneuma

grain by   sin
gle   grain   the   gr
eat wind   lifts   of
f   the dune the   s
and grain by   sin
gle grain   the dune
and every   dune d
oes   die up in   no
t cloud   utters it but
the living   air
cares or no   it carr
ies   unseen   above
thought   vast   de
spair or no   desert
nomad in no tent   in
tent of   sky   s
uch sprits be a   blo
om   or no a broken
key   a still sudden s
till when   stops b
reath breathing   som
e shy   mouth   why
now shut   d
rops on acres   green
whole   deserts   down

Endangered Species

Even this
brief thought is endless. A
man speaks as if unaware of the
erotic life of the ampersand. In the
isolate field he comes to count one by
one the rare butterflies as they
die. He says witness is to say what
you mean as if you mean it. So many
of them are the color of the leaves
they feed on, he calls sympathy a fact, a
word by which he means to make a claim
about grace. I have in my

life said many things I did not
exactly mean. Walk
graceless through the field. Graceless so
the insects leap up into the blank
page where the margins fill
with numbers that speak diminishment.
Absence as it nears also offers astonishment.
Absence riddles even this
briefest thought, here
is your introduction to desire, time's
underneath where the roots root down
into nothing like loose threads
hanging from the weaving's underside.
No one seeing the roots
can guess

at the field above. Green
equation that ends in yellow
occasions. Theory is
insubstantial. The eye latches on
to the butterflies as they fly
and the quick heart follows, not
a root in nothing but a thread across
abstraction. They fly away.
What in us follows we do not name.
What the butterflies pull out us
as in battle horses pull
chariot, we do not

name. But there is none, no battle,
no surge, no retreat, a field
full not of danger, but the endangered,
where dust-wings pull from us
what we thought we lost, what theory
denies, where in us ideas go to die,
and thought with the quaking grass quakes.
Some call it breath but I'm still breathing.
So empty I know I'm not any emptier.
On slim threads they pull it out me,
disperse—no
one takes notes—disappear, &

Ethos & Eros

Ache of my tooth in another's mouth or another's
ache in mine. A form of pain to bear
The riddle of the moral life, the "moral life,"
The skeptical speak with scare quotes in the air,
The "moral life," a kind of idea, or nostalgia,
By which they mean something that isn't there—
Forever, forevermore, but forever ever more
A symptom of the poet's fever or is it what
The poet fears, that word "pain," that word "love,"
Patient in the mouth waiting for pain to arrive,
But it doesn't; waiting for love; or those words
Waiting like patients for the drip to administer
The drug, the impatiens pink and white, white
And pink, small circles in a pot above the sink.

Desire bound chaos to night and then the stars
Began their consideration of influences, light
That pricks the eye but gives the earth no sheen,
Like a breath meant for another's mouth to breathe,
But breath is what shines its bright points in mind,
Small dreams, or constellations, or once upon a time—
A young woman prayed to the lit lamp for love
Nightly the wind blew through her open window
A force she could not see, but could feel, her limbs
Loosening the little knot of nerves called thought
Into darkness, element of the soul's old pleasure,
Where reason dismantles its pride into a pulse
That like a god works itself all by itself, a kind of
Idea like an arrow in the blood, or the magnet's needle.

To pierce the heart's architecture, doubt's sacred
Penetralium. Grammar also possesses the wound
Of which this song speaks, song that is no song,
That rights no wrong, that refuses the object's
Indifference and makes it ask to what it belongs,
Gravity or some other subject, the void, the moon,
Or the man with his hand in his pocket stroking
His instrument while humming a country tune.
An ant carries a seed as large as itself back home—.
The rams sleep in the shadows of the brush—.
A sparrow sings to no one who is not alone—.
Still the lovelorn god scatters blind his poppies
Giving sleep if not oblivion. Some speak in dreams;
Others wake in pain from the wound never given.

Some Rules of Grammar

Like a man searching for what he holds in his hands
I heard inside my head the line like lightning I heard it
But couldn't write it down like thunder should
Come and announce itself from within itself boom
God is hard says the man holding emptiness in his hands

Like a man unstrung by desire that liar string desire
A nerve vibrates untouched by any bow
The body becomes the indirect object humming
The tune it cannot play and what is it to say
A girl in a cloud the goddess swept away

Leaving an antler on an altar in her place longs
Still for the wedding gift of the hero husband's hand—
So old such dreams of the grammar of wanting
The band of nettles and forget-me-nots that bind
The loose hair and fear and wanting fear to return

The vital darkness to what light cut into form
For what against the sun's cruel nominations
Of objects in the indicative mood the moon
Shines reprieve as what might or could have been
Like emptiness searching for a man to hold it

Like thunder that does not know how to speak
Its own name among the vague innocents
Hiding behind citadel walls who want only a sign
To describe fate as death or a different institution
Where the eagle releases the dove and the child

Cries stones for tears and the hero like the moon
Throws down his spear and grows his hair long
And in a spiral of gold binds his black hair tight and tight
Strings the lyre and loosens the sash of his robe
And sings inside the song a hollow for a home

A sorrow for a heart and a loan of small harms
In the blood that others may learn the tune
Word by word the voice works in what it wishes
A name neither grave nor cloud but some other sign
The axe-handle I or I the arrow quivering in ground

Hunt & Hearth

Name them staghorn and fetlock
Name the dogs green eyes in torchlight
Bed of bent grass and gazelle
And the wounded leap highest and hidden spring
Name them white tail and doe ear and blood
Dappled throat and sunlit ruby pulse in the ear and marrow
Name the dogs tendon taut as arrow string strung
Name them bone all of them bone bone

Call the heart rabbit in its hole
Rabbit that sleeps curled up in its ears call it
Deaf to blood's mad rush call it
Senseless when mind spins muscles into fear
And fear digs a little deeper the hole that is its home
Call the heart a rabbit hiding in this hole

String of the lyre and the arrow's string
Both fling out the thought they sing
And make a wound they call a heart
Whose life is pierced when it begins
It begins to feel when it begins to bleed
String of the lyre and the arrow's sting

Deep in the woods where the hounds lope
On the deer path when they lap up the distance
Sped on by names called out behind them
Sprung out from the taut string of their names
Fate plays the same trick again
Naming some after what they become
Naming some what they hunt

He of the pierced ankle named swollen foot
He of stag horns grown out his head

So scarlet the arrowhead is before it's strung
So red the tooth before the bite
Name meat meat and muscle muscle
This smoke on the altar is smoke on the altar
That some pleasure in the clouds inhales
Name hunger after what it hunts when it hunts
Some end to desire or name it nothing
Nothing better than a home built around a fire
Nothing better than a hut

Eclogue

—for Brenda Hillman

The wars gave him my house   he said
That stranger who arrived   taking
What never was mine   my land
Of long grass   and rivulet   and seed
Now I carry on my shoulders this baby
Goat bleating at every step   Lyre, liar ...
Prophet, profit ...   How did that old song go?

> *...a bee flew through the wedding party*
> *gathering...   ...a boy uses the sun to...*
> *...a spider built its web inside a lantern...*
> *...intelligence...   .... drone on remote*
> *control...   ....burn his name in wood...*

There is that trick the mind keeps playing
Inside the eye called beauty   it makes
Things so bright I go blind   there is a trick
Asleep in the fine bones of the ear
One note played on the shepherd's pipe
So long   nearly forever   becomes what is
Silence and   so God hires the mimics
To speculate   even the stars wage their wars

> *...$a^2 + b^2 = c^2$...   ...she carries pollen*
> *on her thighs...   ...the student should*
> *show his work...   ...plant your pears*
> *your children will gather...   ...the proof*
> *kept repeating the same...   ...the work*
> *shows...   ...rock, seashell...   ...error...*

But what can music do   against a soldier?
What can music do   beneath the sun
Where aphids suck the green stalk   and hands
Get older?   The threshing blade wears dull
The hand that bears it   an eye at a distance
Surveils the helpless spring   a button
To press for Arcadia   an arrow on a string

> ...the swans singing will carry...   ...on
> shard harps...   ...your name to the stars...
> ...such crow joy...   ...that star that rings
> ripeness in the grain...   ...to glean...
> ...long since the threshers...   ..and what
> is home...   ...the old constellations ...
> ...abandoned the field...   ...in sky dark night...

There down the road is a grave   there
Just past the control burn   there just
Past the singed grass   just there singing
I'll go   I'll put down the baby   goat
I'd remember the tune if I could   remember
The words   of the goat be careful, he butts
Drive him down to the water   drive him down
To the spring   moss dark green on the stone
Invites any head to dream   that boy long ago
Who tired of the hunt woke up to find the bees
Filled his mouth with honey   the song cannot
Forget itself   in the air   powers are gathering

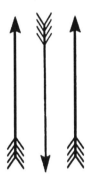

DRONE

sand and what is
sound, the nacre-sound,
this heart's acre, bound, unbound
o irritant speck
all this dust you call clouds
all this doubt you found
just by thinking I am
not quite complete
ly alone o prism o prison
I thought the whole thought
mind the dirt holy ground

DRONE

what is alone cannot
what is a fact alone cannot
what is in the low clovers' slow
thousand-fold stems cannot from poppy
to what poppy is or from rose to what's a
rose cannot self-inflict desire more clear
in words if we did not know it we could not
guess what in fact gathers
the patient field into empty chambers
a worker in the brood nest works what is
alone cannot live

DRONE

less secret wars said:
murkiness rules the limits:
days any drone hit the vast
exempt: death
reported he had been killed:
promise-threshold: a complex
threat: condemned the incoming
relation with the past:
many years since the beginning
times: strike peace
into force but also: kill
the month: killed: wounded: killed:
died: deed: killed thought:
his weapon was peace

DRONE

once I lived in quiet all kind
all kinds of song I once lived
in quiet all of each one of me lived
o worm o mind o yes worm you you
wind silk around the hunger thoughts
patient bind and bide, bide and bind
what sun defines this song denies
this error in the circuit that grinds
as it guides o rut o halo o spiral
of time be calm be quiet as the lost do
doubt it even as it sings o song

DRONE

what honey-heavy portable heaven
requires law to wander law to swarm
to keep beneath the thousands-thick hum
the queen cloaked in royal-scent warm
any hollow can be a home
as when a fact feeling suddenly weightless
leaves in the mind a little room
where the bliss-busy drone might cease to roam
exclude this thought from the hive's whole stress
usefulness dies when command closes
heaven's wax vault and love's honey loan

DRONE

a first drone
rules the troubled known:
it will be uncomfort
able work: stop
and express rain in every
day: stop the
drone ignoring even the
drone: drone
is the vast out-said: drone
of describing as "just"
ever more
transparent sight strict
er rules

DRONE

hear nothing hum
some hum here is nothing's
whole song it lets the sun be
not quite music it lets the sun be dumb
calms nerves in nervous thumb
thinks this blank inside a word
silences what this this is knows
nacres the irritant grain
some call mind
just a pearl just a pearl that learns to
mindless shine

DRONE

even to the exile
whose hunger is his wandering home
the rainbow doubles in height ultraviolet
not peace as promise but prism's violence
kind shatter of white sun's stream
what a drop less then dew can do
in air to air it is the task of the drone
to reunite the mosaic parts o bright bright
flowers of the wondering field wild
to produce in the hole a whole
o drone produce a whole in the mind

DRONE

open a new heart
away from the epic: that day
terror might all
end: approach in drone
the danger: to the: to the
used places: that threat
cannot approach alone the
secret: a day
drone does not drone
desire: draw down
the past and more than time died
in drone: also that now of no
further details: the
world under the veil

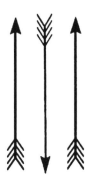

Psalm

I keep deer in my heart
forgive the ancient fold
I keep the woods there too
o altar that wanders
away from prayer keep no
thing blank in this highest
praise deer drink water out
their hooves cloven print

Ode on the Mountain

Caught in the thought-tangled thicket
The ram by its horns grows weary:
How begin to die? A child no longer
A child asks his question to the stone
He sat on waiting. He throws in time.
He throws in the wary mind grown
Weary: watchfulness has its weight:
Astonishments patience dulls into facts
Sourceless and tame: wonder
Followed by a shadow called shame.

*

What first stuns later causes sleep:
The sun, the absent sun:
At the end of the equation, the sum.
How begin to add it up? A man
Only a man says age overcame me:
Not as hound, an hind—
Not as fear, the eye:
But as a sparrow overcomes a crumb
Or as a sparrow settles on the egg she broods:
The answer feels larger than the question.

*

Look down. Those ashes are my shadow
Left on the stone where I did not exactly
Sleep. All those centuries I thought
The work required needs only these few years:

Gentle drift of pronouns, each into each,
Where gradually I wake to the question
How was the night? and say, "It dreamed."
It dreamed. And the next day it went to work.
It fed the children, and it read a book.
At night it washed its face without a look

*

In the mirror. Some vision harms the eye
That sees it. Some song hurts the ears—
Out the rags of the clouds was it a voice
Spoke those red words? *Behold*, it said.
Take who you love most and go, it said,
To the mountains. I carry now
What I carried then: some rope, a bunch
Of sticks tied to my back: a body
Can bear wood enough for the fire
That consumes it. Not much is needed:

*

Just a hand, just a spark. Then I carried
What I carry now: now
It can't be seen, the wood: now
The wood's invisible: the rope a thin line
Coiled around the mind
To hold together what falls apart:
Thought, thought, I thought—
And throat, throat, and some heart
Loose and astray that wants to, but
Cannot mend its way, its prayer: bind me
Tighter. Tighter. Be violent. Give repair.

Prayer

Not only pains and effort but also prayers,
Also prayer-work, and dull muscle ache
Of lifting worry into world and world
Into point, but also density that makes
Ideas surrender to limit and limit
Sorrows, limit keens, limit wants the stars
In burlap sacks seized and wants a stick
To drag across the dirt a line—

Maybe I've forgotten the right way to talk:
Inside my head like a lion the concept
Prowls, hungering after edges
That can't be found, edge fury might find,
Dirt's underside or sky's ground, sedgegrass
Into nothing bound, that leapt over, leapt across,
That driven hungermad by toothblind need
The lion leaps and leaping becomes
The sparrow it chased from the weeds—

This thought of the other world, put it away
In the drawer: maybe in the dark it will grow
Acheless, "like the moon," I want to say,
"Acheless like the moon," and then I remember
The moon is what teaches us aching—
Coinbright thief who cannot steal herself
Away from her condition, pulling tides
Around her shoulders but the aqueous shawl
Shatters when lifted—only when it's fallen

Is it whole. Faith floods the little room
Where I practice faith, time cannot save
This thought, airless tending, God heard
Each prayer before the praying spoke
Urgent in collapse, mind's diamondmine
Gives coal and pressure, counsels patience,
The prayer answers itself, a single Adam
Forever with the fruit in his mouth, not

Swallowed, not sparrowed, not thrushed,
Not warbled, ongoing instant where song
Need not catch up to the fact already of
Being sung, sung, sung, as the moon
By the earth for eternity has been spun,
Past perfect, tense needless of belief,
It has been all of it as it has been, I am
That I am, logic of the ceaseless orbit,
Lion that learns to devour itself, mind

That learns to think, prayer predicts pain
So pain predicts prayer, maybe I forgot
The grammar that's right, I mean just,
A poem only of marks that remind the mind
"Breathe here, and here; breathe here, and here,"
Page missing words like room missing walls
Like field missing grass like a simile all
By itself saying as its prayer, *as is as is—*
Deafen the echo that might say "azaleas."

No one is saying that word here: azaleas.
No one says nightshade, bindweed, mandrake
Nettle, forget-me-not, morning glory. No one
Says nothing. This field, plait by plait,

Unbinds tendril from trellis, petal from light,
Root from stone, eye from sight.
Silence: give each word
Fair warning. The prayer is about to begin:
"   ,   ;   ,   ."

A Century of Meditation

That if I knew how, would I—.
In singing, not to sing—.
Build the thing, or don't—.
God as if God weren't there—.
Prayer as remote control,
as heretic point, as market share—.
Read about the animals:
their eyes that stare into the open,
and there the void-glare glares—.
Where hearts go out—. Ends stop—.

*

Grows so heavy when it grows up.
Knowing less weighs it down.
As arms still carry the burden
just put down, blood carries echo
of the echo of the—. Some sound.
Thought of blood as thought.
What heart doesn't want a master
more clear than itself, less riddled
by the commands: *put down to pick up,*
be abandoned by what is given.

*

Grace is when what need not fall
comes falling. So gently of itself
the snow. So gently of itself the fog.
Blocking at night the stars. A voice
speaks at night above me where it lives,

leaning out the window, wondering
at the moon, how close it is, how near
at hand, a voice could touch it
with its hand. I don't make a sound.
Scared I'll scare the voice from falling down.

*

Mimic, not mock—.
Irony is when no one knows how to laugh.
Mind keeps making itself
its own example—.
Try mine on, it says; my thought.
Leafless oak surrounded by the leafed-out birch.
Then a song. Then some weeks.
Then I learn to think about the clouds
as a mind drifting through its own
humor. Not a joke. The darker leaves uncurl.

*

Not dead, corrupt—
not corrupt, decaying—
the author in the poem of his making.
Urn of his making. Bird of his making.
What sings inside itself, does it sing
in me? Song that waking itself
lulls every other ear to sleep.
And the voices there (in dreams,
without speaking speak; and the eyes there,
seeing they don't see) other voices answer.

"God's not dead"
is a sticker on a truck, a sticker
on the truck says, "By the time you
read this, I will have reloaded,"
an Uzi in silhouette pointing at the words.
I don't know how to think, I think.
A thing done under threat. I imagine
a picture when I read a word. So many things
ache when needs aren't met. Head, aspirin.
Heart, asp. Blood stiff in the member.

*

What is this violence that makes my hands
these hands, blood in, blood on—.
Dream of a cloud dragging a chain across the ground
following the line in the dirt.
Dream of a—. Gun. Stick. Candle. Cloud. Stone.
A child's face lights up the page she reads,
As does the sun, the moon—.
That's a lie. The sun is inside the moon.
The book inside the girl's head, unfolding leaves.
My hands inside the blood inside my hands—.

*

The old man believed in numbers as gods.
He used to be a beautiful courtesan—.
In another life he might have been a dog.
Hammers on anvil taught him the musical ratios.
He drew this portrait of god's face:

Eternal soul—. Stars the pegs drawing music taut—.

*

Beauty and truth—.
I lash myself to the letter I
and listen as the clouds sail by—.
The sirens sing their song
that makes a hole in happiness—.
That source of song—. That hole—.
Doppler effect of the police car
chasing the street. A man
with middle name Storm knocks
on church. The church lets in—. The storm—.

*

On Lesbos the refugees gather on the shore.
Like a strong wind shatters the pine, so love—.
Like a god he seemed to me, sitting near you—.
Where the old poet suffered love others suffer
differently. I think there is no end to thinking.
Doesn't stop—. Doesn't get anywhere—.
I keep treating other voices like the voice of God
who has no voice, who carved a grid in stone.
Maybe I'm being difficult—. Maybe confused—.
Tune without words—. Impossible bird called hope—.

On the Soul

...is always what it is is within
life but life cannot touch it is afraid
or not when fear creeps from distant
shadows over the body is how it is
with intelligence or not of any opinion
the thorn numb or is it dumb what
is sharp but is what feels no pain is
pleasure its solitude or is it like light
woven through a leaf a sympathy in
blood or the erection or a symphony
before the violin string by rosin pulls
the rose through the air or is the rose
of infinite petals the rose of no one's
sleep is the doves in the columbarium
is a nest not an urn not an urn is
a window holding itself open in space
is lost treatise on Atlantis is Atlantis
itself is the horse galloping in a cloud
called thunder or is it in the long grass
the fawn asleep long past her mother
who has gone is a neighbor of wisdom
is a chariot driven by a nameless man
is synapse or cul-de-sac or hollow below
bone is pushing up a hill a boulder is
the boulder rolling down is the eyes
of the Gorgon on a shield or eyes
behind closed lids when the sun lights
pink the skin as it lights a late cloud up
or the lightning lacing the thunderhead
through self-lit self-illuminating self-

corrupting self-destroying is a lion
who has an idea instead of teeth is
a logic that learns to hate the ratios
is a radio tuned to no station is static
is a sock clinging to a shirt in heaven
is a double-knot a careful child ties
loosening all day as she runs is a string
trying to tie itself into a knot is
a purifying machine turning in circles
centripetal in in-cycle centrifuge
is a circumference being apocryphal
centers is arch and note on the y-axis
where in the infinitesimal the meadow
grows wild grows wide and those roots
digging down dangle out the simple
plane hovering there in nothing out past
Pluto reaching backwards to the sun…

Efforts of Translation

What burns becomes ash becomes dust becomes
Clouds that gather together the sea, so the clocks
Carry hours, and later on the bells rain down
What in them rings, not time, but something
That rhymes with time, like fire, or ash, or dust.

You, you also speak. Of ash, of hair, of milk
Gone dark as night. Sometimes God
Crept beneath the hotel door in a crack of light,
Sometimes not. Sometimes nothing at all.
The clouds in the sky sit down on the sea,

The children braid their hair before the mirror
While water fills up the sink. The children
Teach their hands to do this work; later each
Teaches her hands how to fall asleep. Sometimes
At night, sometimes not, sometimes at noon

Or later, in the dark inside the dark, in the night
The lidless stone eye alone can see, the gray stone
Behind the eye that never becomes the world falling
Endlessly into it, the gray zone not made of stone
But of stoniness, where nouns drift into adjectives

And what remains is a powder that whitens
The face from within, some dust within the face,
Time and ash, and the old milk that nursed
Their bones. You speak also. Both of you speak.
My daughters. What I want to hide from you

Hides inside you. To yourselves stay blind
Is the latest prayer. Soon enough it will grow old.
"Know thyself" in the rubble heap
outside the ruins. Lidless eyes that mind the stone.
I mean give it a mind. That crack in the face of the god.

Ritual Version

—for Kate Middleton, Australian poet

humself, shamself, hymnself, shameself—.
lameself, lambself, numbself, unself—.
sing anger, goddess, of—. many devices—.
sing anger godless—. tell me who—.
sacred in the sea suffered so many woes—.
bookshelf, doubtshelf, debtshelf, riftshelf—.
driftshelf, truthshelf, foolshelf, rueshelf—.
sing less the many souls sent—. they perished—.
sing spoils for the dogs—. who swallowed down
the foolish song—. the soul and its compan-
ions—.
nounself, nonceself, nonself, lashself—.
ashself, lawself, thoughtself, aughtself—.
tell me, muse, from any point—. and birds—.
sing less the wrath of—. a man's cleverness—.
tell also us—. of recklessness—. of home—.

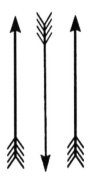

Abecedarian

ox, house   patient animal, patient tool
earth the abstract field where lines intersect
and build a   *throwing stick*   mind, the living
veil pulled aside reveals another   *door*   or
is the apocalypse different now, the letters
all symbols of the hand or   *window*   what
as a deer in the bramble or rabbit under pine
is seen through what the hand builds, that
hook   hanging thoughts on wood
also hangs   *weapons*   none simple, none
simply abstractions, distractions, a   *wall*
built brick by brick to keep out the barbarous
ideals, each letter an idol, an idea, or is it
built to keep them in, as a   *palm*   holds
within its cup the water brought trembling up
to the mouth, thirst a   *goad, water*   a goad
the lambs listless in the late day's heat bleat
softly in their sleep, and you, gentle singer,
gaze down at   *fish*   silent in the stream
dreaming another alphabet, some other
support   for the names you are afraid to say
that being said alter the   *eye*   or in it
build an altar where the old gods go and suffer
reason's speculative heat, that accidental purity,
melting down the gold into the cool   *mouth*
that finds itself when it opens full of needles—
but no mouth finds itself, you'll say, shepherd,
goatherd, technician of the drone, no mouth
is on the   *hunt*   as a hound bounding in
circles after its own tail while the white-tip flame

disappears of the fox in shadow, so many
theories abound, mouth as sanctuary, mouth as
debt, mouth as throne, mouth as   *needle's eye*—
but you can use your   *head*   to do most anything
so different than a   *tooth*   where rough seas
grow calm, where sails a hull full with grain
from Phoenicia, where a volcano erupts its ashy
script across the ancient sky, where at a wedding
party a child cries in fear at the bee clinging
to a cube of ice in the bowl of sweet punch,
where intelligence gathers its powers in the air,
can drag an edge against the throat and leave
no scar, all this the mind can do by pressing
some letters and letting some go, but a tooth
is different, a tooth leaves its   *mark*

Eiresione

—for Martin Corless-Smith

wild deer children
your burden falls on death ears
your monster has more than one eye
carry a branch and sing a song
between door and door
the wider door blooms

⁊

a fig in a non-factual state
hope might hope
grammar in a better mood
a child desires to be given
a wish with a rule you cannot
wish for more wishes

⁊

tie fruit to branch and also
something sweet
discs in yellow wrappers
brighter than the sun
a noose around a slice of cake
governs the crumbs

&&

who is wisest who
is sentenced to death for saying the
sun is hot metal
stars move around earth but not under
gold is made of smaller gold
death writes his little grammar book

&&

oikos nomos
the oracle goes up and down
alive in the house that is a bubble
the child fills in words for thoughts
everything's a test say the gods
all of the above a blank cloud

&&

youth corrupt with new gods
is it exile or is it death Memorex
won't the heart keep its damage
singing all by itself the lyre in the blood
a light on the machine turns red
when infinite loop is pressed

quincunx and burial
urn and facts of false knowledge
the author's skull rests on the books
he wrote in two volumes religio medici
in ash the thief can find no head or hand
but what is buried can be found
by child by dog or by the rut of plow

∂℘

a little happy poem
so sweet in the ear it fills the mouth
this sweetness called the sun
let the mind be gone or just
on the tongue a crumb

∂℘

hemlock   who knows what is
at work in the soul is it happiness
judges use words to judge words
say there is a liar in the blood
the heart a chant that cons desire
into becoming the gods a golden
shower a swan no shame o Europa
a white bull without blemish

wrap the olive branch in wool
hang the flask of oil and the flask of wine
the honey cake and torn vine
this blind man is his own guide
this song a surety on his debt
hostage to the blessing let someone sing
the odd sea I'll add back to the sea

Some Forms of Perpetual Mourning

The child has a music box she calls her "icicle."

When she opens it she says the sun's come home
    which means the ice is melting; the music is the sun.

Wind up the deer and they play a tune
    called fear of the useless wound.

The meadow is a square the scissors cut out
    the dark woods. Owls ask, *Who?*

She carries the hoof of her broken horse in her pocket
    in case another horse needs an extra.

Why do the wolves look up when they cry *How?*
    Because the clouds forgot the name of the moon.

For show and tell she brought a brass doorknob with a dent
    she found on the ground; she calls it god.

For a long time she thought the sun had fallen down
    replaced by a yellow sticky note in the sky.

The moon isn't called the moon any longer the child says;
    then, sitting in the grocery store cart, she howls.

Why, o music box, o mouth;
    none of the emptiness gets more empty.

Apophatic

—for Peter Gizzi

nothing changes nothing
grows wild nothing grows
tame nothing bends weird
the mind-space into shape
of tether and memory of
ankle gone lame the whole
hurt song called irony can-
not know how chaos aches
beneath the facts it wears
for a face the fact of a
blank page being a form
of a map that is a kind of
mask missing a mountain
or a mouth or a marble
pedestal from which the riddle
pours down and you know
a man is the answer *a man*
but nothing changes nothing
bends absence bright into a
silence called paper white
sun circle or solar sail or lonely
wind across vast despair or
blank hope bearing small repair
that this finger I point at
myself answers the question
what is not is everywhere

Middle Ages

Once, I was a child. When did that horizon—.
Once, I was a child; I built a little boat.
It wanders, it wanders—
Blown by breath caught in a sail, toy breath,
Toy sail, out into the unbreathable reach
The center goes, goes wandering, toy boat.

I drifted into the middle ages. Some current
Pushed my little craft into this room
I cannot leave. The same current pushed open
A door floating on an ocean. A leaky door.
Caught in the drift out went the golden age,
Out the silver and out the bronze. Out iron
And out irony. Out went the bright eye's gleam.
Out went the theory of the world as machine.
Out went the candle, and out went the ghost.
The surface deepened when I needed it most.
Deepened, what I needed most. You—

You see it with me. What the center holds.
Light without sun, but light. Some breath,
Some air. A song like a battered spar
Can't guide but shares our situation—
Where door opens only onto other door,
Life's ongoingness of doors, such
Improbable doors, we've drifted in on
To the threshold-condition.

Sibboleth

Each of us has repeatedly our own shibboleth
Husk tight against the ear, against the grain.

Exactly because no one's eyes are wide as the world
We must each say to ourselves the word

And ask if we belong. To the river: do we
belong? To the olive on the twig: Do we?

How often at night the mouth works
Its own words by itself for no one's hearing

Not even our own. Grain sleep of dreams
In which snow again buries the river and fields;

And also, the strange slow green beneath ice
Or in eyes. An "and" that acts like an "or."

And those who in daylight say *No pasarán*
At night let us enter the holy land, the secret,

The cipher that says "I am." Poor river
Flowing endlessly into itself, poor heart—

Babel's bricks break down in the blood
and that Eden tree has a leaf still called a lung.

I carried the pebble of it all in my thought,
I came all this way to sing one song.

Poem

woven nettle and laurel crown
and laurel crown and woven
cloth and thistle down and broken
nettle into garland bound
and something unexpected:
a bead, a jewel, a fragrant cloth
in the grass abandoned, a moth
and a moth, and a month, or a mouth,
or is it a month, yes, all torn out,
when to open a door drops
the dusty wings to the ground
in their stupid clamor among
what else I forgot: logic's knot,
a thought between consecutive
wounds, or the wound, a wound
between these thoughts: this child
that lets the baby doll drop
and says to it now, now, now
you're asleep, now the baby's asleep:
a grass pillow and a grass bed and
the apple tree's tympanum waiting
for a little wind and a little wind
posts the useless news: the sun
has not yet, not yet, been removed.

Notes

Theseus's Ship—the source for the poem can be found in Plutarch's *Life of Theseus*.

Eclogue—is based on Virgil's lovely Eclogue IX.

Drone—the series moves three times through three different approaches: first, *drone* as constant sound, chant, or form of prayer; second, *drone* as worker bee; third, *drone* as weapon. In the latter poems, each is constructed as an erasure from news articles in the *New York Times* or *Washington Post* describing drone attacks in the summer of 2013.

Prayer—begins with a line from Leibniz.

A Century of Meditation—the old man who "believed in numbers as gods" is Pythagoras.

Abecedarian—the italicized words are the English translations of the letters of the Phoenician alphabet, each a kind of picture or ideogram. This language provided the source for Ancient Greek, who kept the order, but abstracted both the letters and their meaning into far more flexible, if less totemic, forms.

Eiresione—refers to a ceremony in ancient Greece in which branches and olive flasks, cakes and other morsels, often wrapped in wool, were carried about by boys who arrived at one's doorstep bearing both these gifts and their song. In some accounts, Homer is said to have enjoyed joining the boys as they wandered and sang. Each small poem I imagine as a little gift wrapped in wool.

Sibboleth—the Hebrew word, *shibboleth*, originally refers to a plant containing grain (ear of corn, head of wheat) and, alternately, a river, stream, or torrent. In a battle against the Ephraimites, as the defeated army retreated across the river Jordan, the tribe of Gilead had each person pronounce the word "shibboleth." The men from Ephraim, unable to pronounce the sh of the word, said "sibboleth" and so were slaughtered.

Acknowledgments

I owe many thanks to the editors who first allowed these poems onto their pages: *American Literary Review, The Literary Review, Gulf Coast, Kenyon Review, The Academy of American Poets Poem-a-Day, Salamander, Harvard Review, INK, Company, Blackbox Manifold (UK), New American Writing, Volta, OAR, Washington Square Review, Miracle Monocle, Bomb, Crazyhorse* and *The Nation*.

Martin Corless-Smith's generous vision in his chapbook series *Free Poetry* gathered together a number of these efforts in *Drone & Other Poems*.

"Apophatic" was included in the *Best American Poetry 2017*. Many thanks to Natasha Trethaway for her kindness in selecting it.

As always, maybe more than ever, I'm in the debt of friends and poets whose vision guides my own. Thank you to Suzanne Buffam, H.L. Hix, Kristen Case, Christina Davis, Brian Teare, Peter O'Leary, G.C. Waldrep, Karla Kelsey, Rusty Morrison, Louann Reid, Ann Gill, Del Harrow, Sanam Emami, Rebecca Beachy, Matthew Cooperman, Aby Kaupang, Camille Dungy, Bruce Bond, Nic Brown, Mai Wagner, Sergio Vucci and Daniel Stolar, whose patient reading and large support opened fertile ground. I owe long gratitude to Lyn Hejinian, Peter Gizzi, Forrest Gander, Donald Revell, and James Galvin. Lastly, to those who have read each poem and syllable: thank you Sasha Steensen, Srikanth Reddy, Martin Corless-Smith, Katie Paterson, and Sally Keith.

Dan Beachy-Quick is the author of six books of poetry, six chapbooks (two in collaboration with Srikanth Reddy), and two prose collections, as well as criticism and fiction. His work has won the Colorado Book Award, and has been longlisted for the National Book Award. He has been a finalist for the William Carlos Williams Prize and the PEN/USA Literary Award in Poetry, and included in the Best American Poetry anthology. He is the recipient of a Lannan Foundation residency, and has taught at the Iowa Writer's Workshop. He was one of two Monfort Professors at CSU for 2013-2015, and his work has been supported by the Woodberry Poetry Room at Harvard University and the Guggenheim Foundation. He is a University Distinguished Teaching Scholar at Colorado State University, where he serves as assistant chair of the English Department and teaches in the MFA Program in Creative Writing.

Also by Dan Beachy-Quick

Poetry	*Variations on Dawn and Dusk*
	North True South Bright
	Spell
	Mulberry
	This Nest, Swift Passerine
	Circle's Apprentice
	gentlessness
Collaborations	*Work From Memory: In Response to In Search of Lost Time by Marcel Proust* (with Matthew Goulish)
	Conversities (with Srikanth Reddy)
Chapbooks	*Apology for the Book of Creatures*
	Shields & Shards & Stitches & Songs
Essays	*Of Silence & Song*
	A Whaler's Dictionary
	Wonderful Investigations: Essays, Meditations, Tales
	A Brighter Word than Bright: Keats at Work
Novel	*An Impenetrable Screen of Purest Sky*

Library of Congress Catalog-in-Publication data available upon request.
ISBN: 978-1-946482-30-3

First edition: July 2020.

Cover and text designed by Bill Kuch.

Tupelo Press
P.O. Box 1767, North Adams, Massachusetts 01247
(413) 664–9611 / editor@tupelopress.org / tupelopress.org

Tupelo Press is an award-winning independent literary press that publishes fine fiction, nonfiction, and poetry in books that are a joy to hold as well as read. Tupelo Press is a registered 501(c)(3) nonprofit organization, and we rely on public support to carry out our mission of publishing extraordinary work that may be outside the realm of the large commercial publishers. Financial donations are welcome and are tax deductible.